Preface

My Lord has given me words of life
as I have walked through the cares of this life
and trials that have been like fire.

I have found that in the midst of the process,
the fires, the tribulation,
the Master was beside me enabling me to walk this path.

His arms have embraced me
when I was overwhelmed by circumstances.
His sweet presence integrated every hour of my life.

For His intent is to bring us forth as gold tried in the fire.

Your way, O God, is in the sanctuary; who is so great a God as our God?
Psalm 77:13 NKJV

Oh Lord, let Your mighty anointing arise
within me,
and may I step
back
and give way to Your beloved indwelling Spirit.

I acknowledge You as Lord
of every detail of my life
for You have brought me through the fire;
yet, my garments do not even smell of smoke.

You have brought me up to the high ground
and into a broad place.
I behold a lavish feast prepared before me.

Oh, who is like You, oh God, King of the universe?
The stars and planets were placed in order
by the words of Your mouth.
How much more valuable are the words You speak to me!
Who am I to be Your child, my King?

Have You not said that You will never leave
nor forsake
nor embarrass me?

Truly, I lean upon You,
for You are a strong tower
that I run to in times of trouble.
I shall not be afraid of anything
the world tries to put upon me.

Let God arise within this earthen temple and may His enemies be scattered!

> And there appeared a great wonder in heaven;
> a woman clothed with the sun, and the moon under her feet,
> and upon her head a crown of twelve stars.
> Revelation 12:1 KJV

You have filled up with
    My Word and My Spirit.

        Therefore, I stir the gifts within you
        as I stirred the waters of Bethesda.

Like a volcano,
    you have been seeping the flow
    of My Spirit within,
        but be prepared
        and do not be surprised
            when this internal volcano erupts.
My power shall flow forth beyond measure
    for the day of the Lord is at hand.

        You have purchased gold tried in the fire,
        and you are clothed by My own hand.
            You have anointed your eyes with the salve of My Spirit
            so that you might look
                into the depths of My heart.

*I have placed a garland upon your head,
for I purchased you upon the cross*
                                          with a crown of thorns.
*You see — I have exchanged your carnal mind
for My own mind.*

*There are twelve stars within this garland,
representing My perfect order.*

    So bring forth from the hidden manna and the deep well within.
                              Let Me flow
                                    bringing new life
                                    and hope
                                          to the nations.

> Listen to the Wind Words, the Spirit blowing through the churches.
> Revelation 3:22 TMB

*The wind of God in gale force
is blowing through His anointed vessels of honor,
those who have purchased gold
tried in the fire of discipline.
Their garments are new,
fresh
and white,
with the purity of the Most High.
And My wind is blowing through My people.
My wind pours water
upon the thirsty, seeking heart
and nourishes the hungry.
All who seek,
all who lift up their eyes
shall behold their God—the King altogether lovely and righteous,
the One seated upon the throne.*

*Your eyes will see a door open in Heaven
and the glory of the Lord.
You will look upon the Lamb slain just for you and for many.
No sin was too great,
no offense too grand
that He will not forgive.*

You have purchased garments of My purity,
   of My righteousness.
      For I will keep your name written in the book of life.

As your eyes of understanding are opened,
      you realize that you are no longer in the outer court,
          but find yourself
            in the Holy of Holies.

There the only light is from Me,
     as My radiance
     penetrates your heart.
         You have cast aside all rights to yourself
         and put your life into My loving hands.

And the wind blows and you are no longer.
      All you are aware of is the One perfect
              and true,
        the One seated upon the throne.
And you fall upon your knees and cry,
   "Holy! Worthy is our God!"

> For this reason I, Paul, the prisoner of Jesus Christ . . .
> Ephesians 3:1 NKJV

May I not be as Moab resting on her dregs,
    but may I be emptied of self
        that You might refill me
    with Your life,
            my Lord.

I long to fall into the ground
and die to my own self will
    that Your tree of life might come forth.

Is it not through the pain
and suffering of losing myself
    that I open my heart to receive all of You?
        Yes, even the suffering love.
Help me, my Lord,
    to wait upon You
    and to step out
        in total abandonment
            as I feel Your strong arms lead me
            in Your perfect will.

I am pleased to find myself in Your cell block,
    Your prison of surrender;
        as I relinquish my all unto Your perfect image.

I watch in wonder as I witness my uniqueness
crushed
and broken
and I become pressed
into Your perfect life.

Yes, I give You free dominion of this life I called my own,
for I know full well that I am nothing
until You possess all of me.

As Rachel hid her precious idols,
I also have corners
and hidden crevices of sin
buried
under
the covering
of my unique nature and self-justification.

As I offer all unto You, my King,
may I say as the Apostle Paul, "I am a prisoner of Jesus Christ."

Yet, I have this peculiar freedom,
this strength
that no weapon may penetrate.

> My grace is sufficient for you,
> for My strength is made perfect in weakness.
> 2 Corinthians 12:9 NKJV

My Lord,

Thank You for placing a stake or thorn within me
to hold me to Your purpose.
You, my King, know every dimension of me —
even the depths of my heart.
Yes, I take pleasure in infirmities,
in distresses,
in reproaches
for Christ's sake.
For truly when I am weak,
You are strong.

Therefore, I exchange my strength for Yours
and lean upon
Your power and grace
every hour of the day.

I sit down under Your shadow
for You are as a tree laden with abundant fruit,
and Your fruit is my delight.

The times and the seasons of Your will, who can comprehend?

I rest in the knowledge that all things coming into my life —
the bad
and even the good —
are sifted through Your majestic hands.

Yes, the enemy will prowl about as a roaring lion
        but he can do only what You allow, my King.

For I have entered into the fellowship of Your suffering.
    I have been through the wine press,
        and You are drinking with enjoyment
            the fruits of my submission.
    I have accepted with great joy my destiny.

You tell me that I am Your dove and undefiled one
    for we have become
        one
in the fellowship of Your suffering.

Yes, my Love, I cannot trust in my own reasonings
    because You always have
        a divine, eternal purpose
        for these adversities.
It's during the raging storms that the eagle
        soars to the higher realms.
You have made me as the eagle,
    and we rise
        as one
            above circumstances.

> He reveals the deep and secret things.
> Daniel 2:22 AMP

May I open my mind
to tap into the wisdom of eternity, my King,
    waiting upon You
    and seeking You
        as silver,
    searching for You
        as hidden treasure.

Grant me quick understanding, my Lord,
    for I long to plunge into
    the deep waters of Your Word.

You offer me
    plenteous and difficult-to-fathom truths,
    wisdom as a gushing stream,
        sparkling,
        fresh,
        pure and life-giving
            as I stand face to face
            with the Lord of eternity.

You impart to me words of life
as You embrace me with Your great love,
        and more clearly my eyes are opened
            to the length,
              height,
              depth and
              breadth of You,
                      perceiving,
                      recognizing and
                      understanding
                the wonders of Your person.

Now I understand why it was necessary for me to share Your sufferings
                    as I died daily.
I constantly presented myself upon the altar of sacrifice.

      But look!
           I have laid hold of You
           and You have made me Your own.

> Where has your beloved gone, O fairest among women?
> ... He feeds his flock among the lilies.
> Song of Solomon 6:1, 3 NKJV

If you press through the portals of your own reasoning,
and run after Me with every thread of your being,
then you will have fed
from the King's table.

Oh yes, My lamb, I have buried a shovel
within your hungry, seeking heart,
and I draw you to dig
for the hidden treasures of My Word.

And, as you seek,
you will evermore come into the knowledge
and fullness of the godhead.

I have placed within your heart
eyes to open your understanding
to My unlimited depths.
Yes, your eyes will be opened to the fullness of My body
and your desires will be to grow up,
to mature with all the saints
into one body,
consecrated and set apart for your Master.

You began this walk stumbling like a child
and progressed to a steady gait.
Now, you run after Me,
panting as the deer or young hart.
You notice that your feet are skipping upon the mountain of spices
as I open fresh revelation unto you.

Yes, I draw you.
Run after Me
and feed at My table.

**So Jesus said to them, "Can the friends of the bridegroom fast while the bridegroom is with them?"
Mark 2:19 NKJV**

Do not fast when the Bridegroom is with you, My child,
    for only I call you to a fast
        at My appointed time,
                and I am with you now.

            Yes, I am in you
            and you are in Me
            as you align yourself
            to My perfect will.

Man would tell you to do many things,
    and you would become worn out
        laboring in the vineyards of well-meaning brothers.

        But I call you aside to abide in Me,
            the Living Vine.

You gain life and nourishment from Me.

Would the clay rise up in rebellious self-will and cry unto the potter, "How could you make me so?"

There is the secret place of the Most High
            where you will find true rest.
There is a safe place
        as you are surrounded by My angels.
        Only a few strive by obedience to enter this.

I watch over you with a jealous love, My child,
    and if you are obedient
        then your entire life shall be a fast,
            for it is holy
            and acceptable unto Me.
                It is My life.

Thus says the Lord G<small>OD</small> to these bones,
"Behold, I will cause breath to enter you that you may come to life.
. . . and you will know that I am the L<small>ORD</small>."
Ezekiel 37:5, 6b NASB

Lord, may pride not accompany me to my knees
as I seek Your lovely face.
May we be as one, my Lord —

as Enoch who walked with You
but was not.

Do Your perfect will within me
and in this world
with or
without
me.
But if it please You to use me,
I will wait for Your perfect timing, my King.

For You are Lord,
and I stand before You
as Your humble servant,
crushed and broken,
for Your highest purpose.

Only the pressed juice and poured-out wine are pleasing to the King.

So very often I must slay the giant of my wretched ego
        to fulfill Your desires in my small life.

I must constantly press through the crowds of thoughts
        and preconceived ideas
    to bow before You
        and touch the hem
        of Your fullness.

The Holy Spirit hovers over the deep within my soul
    and dispels the darkness of self-will,
        and I can hear You say, "Let there be light!"

> Up to the present, we know, the whole
> created universe groans in all its parts
> as if in the pangs of childbirth.
> Romans 8:22 NEB

Lord, I sense a groaning in the Spirit
as the old creation
or the established church
travails as a woman giving birth.

For You are the God of Abraham,
or faith,
the God of Isaac,
or promise,
and the God of Jacob,
or change.

You do a new thing in this day
as You change all who are willing to seek Your face
with every aspect of their being.

I observe that You have clothed Your church
with the radiance of the Son of God,
and along with the old creation
they declare the glory of the King.

Oh, who is like You, oh Lord?
For You crown the woman with a garland of twelve stars.

The old creation reflects the radiance of the Lord
as she brings forth new life.
This new many-membered son
reflects the light of the morning star.
Did you not exchange Your thorny crown
for this finished work
in purchasing Your own?

My King, as the man-child comes forth,
I see these are Your remnant,
those who abandoned all
to seek Your face.

You catch us up to the very throne room
and no fierce enemy may devour us.

> For lo, the winter is past, the rain is over and gone.
> The flowers appear on the earth;
> The time of singing has come.
> Song of Solomon 2:11, 12 NKJV

*The winter is only
to prepare you for spring, My child.
It may seem long and severe
as the north winds of tribulation
freeze the very core of your self-worth.*

*But there comes a time when the painful north wind
must give way
to the flowers of spring.*

*The mountains that loomed before you
must melt and
swell the streams of living water
flowing through you
from the very heart of God.*

*Oh yes, the south wind is gentle and yet forceful,
for is it not the breath of God
bringing forth new life
from our graves of despair?*

Let the river flow, My child,
    and watch the Spirit take total control of you
    as you blossom forth with all the chief spices.

        A garden enclosed is My beloved
        and you have been long in the dark ground.

                But this is the time to give forth
                the scent and beauty of your Beloved.

For I hover over you
as the Husbandman tending His prized possession,
                His garden of delight.

    Let Me eat of your pleasant fruits, My love.

> Are your ears awake?
> Listen, listen to the Wind Words,
> the Spirit blowing through the churches.
> Revelation 2:11 TMB

My Lord, You stand before us
with tears in Your eyes
   as You wait for Your precious ones
      to come apart
      and seek
         Your lovely face.

I can hear Your knocking
upon the doors of men's hearts
   as they go about
   running to and fro,

      oblivious to the wind words
      that blow through You
       to bring life,
       healing,
       refreshing
       and hope.

Oh, the wind of Your Spirit blows across this land.
Who will turn his face into the wind
  and set his face like a flint
  in order to run after You?

    For I have tasted of You, my King, and You are good.
    My soul and my hungry spirit only cry for more,
      for I cannot get enough of You.
    I am overwhelmed by the unknown limits within You.

Who can search,
* and find,*
*   and absorb the heights,*
*   depths,*
*   and fullness*
*   of Your Spirit?*

As with Moses, You call us to turn aside and see this strange thing —
* yes, the very fire of Your being burns within us*
*   as it consumes the wood, hay and stubble of our busyness.*

I realize that I have become black as the tents of Kedar
* for I have labored in the field of my own desires*
*   and my selfish ways.*

Now You offer me the radiance of Your glory
*   as You crown me with new life.*

Oh, My Lord, I will hold You and never let You go!

> This is what the LORD says to the men of Judah
> and to Jerusalem;
> "Break up your unplowed ground
> and do not sow among thorns.
> Circumcise yourselves to the LORD,
> circumcise your hearts . . .
> Jeremiah 4:3,4a NIV

Oh, the plow of God, my Lord,
Oh, the plow
    that roots up every idle and high thing
        that exalts itself against the perfect will of God
    in my life.

I can feel the sharp blade of Your Spirit,
    working,
    digging within me
            as You cast away the stones of yesterday
            and prepare me for new life
                and higher realms.

I remember that the fallow ground remains the same
    as fruit follows the plow.
        I may praise You for the victory in this painful process.
        I choose not to drink from the bitter waters of lethargy.

My King, I finally submit to the plow
and watch Your mighty hand carefully.
        Yes, carefully plant new mysteries within the ground
                of my very soul.

Come reapers,
*   come and pick the fruit within this garden of the King.*
*   For I have sunk my roots deep*
*   within the fullness of my Lord.*

He has called me the pleasant planting of His own heart
*   and He has caused me to be the garden of the Lord.*

I find myself enclosed by His manifest presence
*   as He calls His beloved ones*
*   to partake of the fruit thereof.*

For this is indeed the season of harvest.

> I saw the Lord sitting on a throne,
> high and lifted up,
> and the train of His robe filled the temple.
> Isaiah 6:1 NKJV

My Lord,

You are high and lifted up
as You stand before us
in all radiance and glory.

I look upon Your face
and see Your eyes
as flames of fire
piercing my very soul.

Your hair is white as wool
portraying that You are indeed
the Ancient of Days
and all wisdom.

But Your voice, my King,
Your voice is as
the sound of many waters.

Oh yes, my Lord,
Your body is composed of many saints
of Your very own,
and we are like streams of living water
as we allow You to flow
through us.

When we are fully submitted to You,
        Your countenance is like the sun
                shining in full power
                      at midday.
                            For You are the light of the world,
                            and You have placed that fire
                                  within us
                            along with the two-edged sword
                                  of Your powerful Word.

We can see that our feet glow as brass or fine bronze
        for we have walked through the furnace
        and been refined.

    My Lord,
                I stand in awe of You
                as You sustain and cherish
                            Your body of chosen ones.

> But those who wait for the Lord—who expect,
> look for and hope in Him—
> shall change and renew their strength and power;
> they shall lift their wings and mount up [close to God]
> as eagles [mount up to the sun];
> they shall run and not be weary;
> they shall walk and not faint or become tired.
> Isaiah 40:31 AMP

I have caused you to soar as the eagle
unto
heights
unknown.

For you have turned your face into the wind of My Spirit
and I have lifted
you
even into the throne room
of the Most High.

Yes, you have chosen to make your home in the jagged cliffs of the rock
where I feed you hidden manna
and revelation
upon revelation.

Now you understand why I first must hold the seven stars,
which is my completed and mature bride,
in the palm of My hand.

You see, I must feed you from My right hand
and fill you with My Spirit,
My life and
My glory.

Then, My child, I cause you to glow as the seven lampstands.
Truly you radiate as a light in this dark world,
for the Light of the World shines through you
as I walk among you.

I have filled your vessel with oil.
Now you must tip this full vessel of your life
and pour out upon My sheep.

Pour out.
Pour out, and when you need fresh oil,
come aside and rise again into My right hand.
And I will refill you as you soar
unto Me.

> The LORD is my rock and my fortress and my deliverer;
> My God, my strength, in whom I will trust;
> My shield and the horn of my salvation,
> my stronghold.
> Psalm 18:2 NKJV

So softly,
    You come to me in the night, my Lord.
So softly,
    You cover me with Your pinions, Your shield.
        For You, oh Lord, are a glorious shield—
          yes, a strong fortress about me.
          And Your glory lifts
          my downcast head.

In this cloud of glory,
    You speak to me of the mysteries of Your heart,
    and we walk together
        as Enoch once walked and fellowshipped
          with the great I AM.
And there is healing in each step we take.

Is not this Your own unique way in which You heal my reproaches,
        infirmities
        and distresses?

How like You, my King,
*   not to use the hand of man as a vessel of healing for me.*

Oh yes, Your precious vessels are Your delight,
*   but most fail to see*
*   that they are submitted to*
*   the wind of the Spirit*
*   blowing through them.*

For we are not our own,
*   and I am pleased with Your possessive*
*   and protective love.*

You have caused me to rejoice in all circumstances
*   for You are in total control.*

> For as the rain comes down, and the snow from heaven,
> and do not return there, but water the earth, and make it
> bring forth and bud,
> that it may give seed to the sower and bread to the eater,
> so shall My word be . . . it shall not return to Me void, . . .
> it shall accomplish what I please.
> Isaiah 55:10, 11 NKJV

Pleasant fruit you have become, My child.
I planted you in My garden
and tended you as you grew.
How I delight to plant the tender seed of a life
into the prepared furrow.

I watched you dig up the fallow ground of yesterday,
and when you sought Me with your entire heart,
mind
and strength,
I tenderly placed you in the ground to wait.

In due season you came forth.
First the blade,
then the bud,
the blooming flower,
and then fruit.

I send the rains of the Spirit to water the earth
    as My tender plants drink
    until they are filled.

You notice that My words are placed in your mouth
        as you drink of Me.
These words do not return void, empty,
    or without fruit
        because you and I are the gardens
        and you are enclosed within Me.
    The words you speak now bring forth new fruit.

We come to this garden to watch the new plantings
and tend the new fruit
    as the deep within them rises
    to the deep within Me.

**Let's keep a firm grip on the promises that keep us going.
He always keeps his word.
Hebrews 10:23 TMB**

*Have I not caused you to soar with Me, My child?
Have we not soared in the heavens as one
as I lift
you far
above
any circumstances?*

*That is why you freely take pleasure in infirmities,
in reproaches,
in needs,
in persecutions and
in distress
for My sake.*

You have learned through the years to put all things in My lap
and let Me comfort you.

How I delight in your total dependence
as you lean upon Me
and continue to cast all
upon Me.
You have found the secret to casting your cares upon Me
for I wait for all My children
to relinquish adversities and burdens
to Me.

I am the burden bearer.

Do not ever cast away your confidence
for it brings great reward.
Be assured that you will receive the promises.

Remember that hope deferred
makes the heart grow faint,
but when it is fulfilled,
it is a tree of life!

Hold fast!
Hold fast to the confession of your hope without wavering
for I am faithful.

Then, My child,

we shall soar as the eagle to heights unknown.

> Let your light so shine before men,
> that they may see your good works and
> glorify your Father in heaven.
> Matthew 5:16 NKJV

The day for the few is at hand.
Some are called to the masses
as the many sinners are saved,
but I cause you to be My Gideon's three hundred.
You are called to be My mighty men of war.
For with Me, you are a majority.
You are one with Me.
I in you,
you in Me.

I have caused you to become My beacon to the world.
You shine forth as a small diamond
but impossible to miss afar off.

You are an example of My strength,
not yours,
as you reflect the Light of the World.

Solidify,
make strong your foundation
as you look only to Me
and remain one in Me.

This will seem unusual to the world,
but I do a new thing with you.

Just surrender all, faint not,
and see what your Mighty God will do!

**I will give to you the treasures of darkness
and hidden riches of secret places.
Isaiah 45:3 NKJV**

*Because you have pressed into Me,
because you have chosen
    to seek the depths of My heart,
        I will show you treasures hidden from the world.
        I will unfold My manifold wisdom
            as you sit at My feet
            and learn of Me.*

*You are indeed the peculiar and unique planting of the Lord.
    As you rise in wisdom,
        knowledge and understanding
            with Me,
        your roots sink deeper
    into the fellowship of My sufferings.*

*Yes, My child, I have torn you,
            but I will heal you.
You are stricken by the adverse circumstances that I allow,
        but I lovingly bind you up by My own hands.*

*Though you sit by the waters of captivity,
do not lay down your harps,
            but lift up your eyes.
        I will open the heavens to you and reveal My glory.
            For I am your true captor
            and you are My prized possession.*

I will never let you go, My child, for you are truly gold tried in the fire.

> Write the vision and make it plain on tablets,
> that he may run who reads it.
> Habakkuk 2:2 NKJV

I can only see this vision, my Lord,
by the light of Your countenance.
It is so very plain,
for Your Word is a lamp unto my feet.

My feet walk in this world and stir up the dust.
Humanity is but dust,
but Your Word stirs up Your people.

You told Peter, "I have only to wash your feet so that you can be a part of Me."
Therefore, I must be cleansed by the living water of Your Word.

Lord, You are cleansing us of the things of this world.
Not only do You stir humanity by Your words,
but You wash the filth of this earth from me.

For I walk in the kingdom,
yet my feet run through the busyness,
the things that would distract,
the good that would rob me
of Your best.

Oh yes, I run,
*   for You have given me a vision,*
*   and without it the people perish.*

Therefore, I keep a firm grip on the vision
*   for is it not Your promise,*
*   the secret intents and desires of Your heart,*
*   for all mankind?*
*   Is it not life*
*   and fresh hope for those drowning*
*   in the sea of despair?*

*   Faith is our hands on what we can't see.*
Therefore, I will hold Your vision and Your promise
*   as I run hand in hand*
*   with You.*

> Bring all the tithes into the storehouse,
> that there may be food in My house.
> Malachi 3:10 NKJV

Do not rob Me, My child,
    for I stand at the door of your heart
        and wait.
            I wait to inhabit you
                as you ascend the hill of My presence
                with your worship and prayers.

Oh, how I long for My own to come up higher in communion with Me.
    I long to feed you from the King's table
        and hold you so tenderly with My right hand as you dine.

        At My table there is great abundance for all
        and rest from your labors.

You, My beloved, are My tithe
        and your worship is a pleasing sacrifice unto Me.
        You become immersed in Me
        as I am your storehouse,
            your all in all,
            your everything.
    Then I will bring food into your house.

Yes, I am your daily bread,
your hidden manna and fresh revelation.

Watch Me open the windows of heaven
as I pour out the new oil and wine.

My mercies are new every morning,
and the dawn or doorpost of your heart must be marked with sacrifice.
Yes, the sacrifice of praise,
worship
and prayer
is pleasing to Me.

And all nations will call you blessed
for you will be a delightful land
where you shall dine with the King
all the days of your life.

> How lovely is Your tabernacle, O LORD of hosts!
> My soul longs, yes, even faints for the courts of the LORD.
> Psalm 84:1, 2 NKJV

When the Ark of the Covenant was brought before the statue of Dagon, the god of the Philistines,
    it fell and smashed to the ground.
              Indeed, it fell on its face
                    before the representative of God's presence
                        and its hand fell upon the threshold.
The house of Dagon had become the house of God.

    The Lord tells us that we stand at the door of His house
    as we freely approach the throne of the Most High.

    The evil Philistines would not even step upon the threshold
    for they saw the power of God.

    As Dagon lay face down before the presence of God,
        so do I, my King,
        lie face down before You
                    in holy reverence and awe.
        I worship You with all that I am
        and ever will be.

May my intellect and pride which invade my head
    fall to the ground in obeisance before You,
        as my feeble works that are not God-ordained
        wait night and day upon Your door or threshold.

    You are the door, my Lord,
        and a day in Your presence
        is as a thousand years.

        No good thing will You withhold from me
            as the radiance of Your presence is all about me.

    For I am a doorkeeper in Your house.

**Weeping may endure for a night,
but joy comes in the morning.
Psalm 30:5 NKJV**

*Oh, my Lord, You have looked upon me in my distress.
I have passed through the valley of Baca or weeping
                      as I make lamentation and mourn before You.*

              But have You not said, "Blessed are those who mourn"?

*But look!
        I see You leaping upon the mountains of separation
                                    to deliver me.
Oh, my King, You have walked me through the dark valley,
        but You deliver me at the breaking of the day.*

        *Like the gazelle, You swiftly came to me in my troubles
            and You lift
                me
                to Your breast.*
*You whisper unto me
that my barrenness of winter is passed.
                The fierce pelting rain is over and gone
                as I blossom forth as the planting of the Lord.*

For the harsh rain becomes a pool of fresh water to reflect Your face.

*You've even caused me to pour forth
                as a spring of living water
                upon the parched waste places of my life.*

                *I have gone from strength to strength
                as Your glory rests upon me.*

*Yes, You lift me above this life
        and hide me in the cleft of the rock,
    in the secret place of the Most High.*

I can hear Your love calling, "Rise up, My fair one, and come away with Me."

Blow the trumpet in the land.
Jeremiah 4:5 NKJV

You, My child,
*   are the instrument on which I play.*
*   You are as the silver trumpets of the priests of Israel*
*   for you trumpet the clear clarion sound*
*   of My heart.*

The silver speaks of My redemptive covering,
*   My blood.*

As the silver trumpets were beaten and hammered work
*   so have you been pressed in on all sides.*
*   Your flesh has been conquered*
*   so that only My Spirit shines forth as the radiance of the sun.*

I can hear your heart's cry: "Come pale horse of death and ride through my life."
*   You know that your flesh must perish*
*   in order for My Spirit to take full control*
*   of this peculiar instrument.*
For I long to make you My instrument of glory.

Therefore, speak a word in season,
*   sing the songs written upon My heart strings,*
*   proclaim My word,*
*   shout from the housetops,*
*   whisper My rest and peace,*
*   declare My desire.*

*   Allow the deep within to flow forth*
*   and proclaim the acceptable year of the Lord!*

> Let us not become weary in doing good,
> for at the proper time we will reap a harvest
> if we do not give up.
> Therefore, as we have opportunity,
> let us do good to all people,
> especially to those who belong to the family of believers.
> Galatians 6:9,10 NIV

Have I not told you, "Pick up your bed and walk"?
I have restored health to you and healed your wounds.
The winter of suffering is gone.

Now the bed that you pick up is Me.
It is My finished work on Calvary,
for I paid the price to make you whole.

Your bed speaks of the Sabbath rest
which is Me.

For I am Lord of the Sabbath and I say unto you,
"Come unto Me all you who are weary, and I will give you rest."

Pick up, manifest My life
as I live and reign within you.
It is my joy and good pleasure to give you the kingdom,
for the kingdom of heaven is at hand.

It is now.
It is finished.

You must walk within Me —
    a brand new, victorious, many-membered son of man within the earth.
        For those who wait upon Me
        and embrace My life
                shall exchange their lives for Mine.
    They shall run within Me,
      skipping over the mountains of adversity,
      and not grow weary in well-doing,
        for it is the season to reap.

      Walk also within Me
      and you shall not grow faint
      for you soar in the Spirit as the eagle.

You are caught up unto Me
and I feed you hidden manna from on high.

> O my dove, that art in the clefts of the rock,
> in the secret places of the stairs, let me see thy countenance.
> Song of Solomon 2:14 KJV

Oh my Lord,
    as I behold You,
    as I gaze upon Your glory,
        I perceive that You are in the secret place of the stairs
        for You are constantly leading me
            higher unto Your chambers.

    I am progressively coming into
    a deeper knowledge and revelation of You, my King,
        as I draw closer
            and closer
                to Your presence.

At times it seems as though we are climbing some rocky slope or secret stairs
        as I ascend unto You
        and You bring me
            from glory to glory.

    You long to hear my voice in praise and adoration
        unto my beloved King.

I see that around Your throne is the emerald of the breastplate of the high priest
    that represents the tribe of Judah or praise.

    Indeed, my Lord,
        You are enthroned in the praises of Your people.

    And it is my joy,
        my delight,
        to join in one accord with the host of heaven
        and sing praises unto the King of Kings,
            my Master,
                my Lord and
                    my Friend.

> "If I then, your Lord and Teacher, have washed your feet,
> you also ought to wash one another's feet."
> John 13:14 NKJV

*You have woven servanthood
within the fabric of my heart,
my King.*

*For I have watched You cleanse my feet
from the cares and bondages of this world.*

*You have called me to walk in the world
but to be not of the world.*

*Your cleansing power washes me from
all of my yesterdays,
all of my preconceived ideas and
all of my ambitions.*

*I cannot walk the path that You have prepared for me
unless
I yield and humble myself before You
and before my brothers.*

*Therefore, I do not take up my intellect or my creative ideas,
but I gird myself with the towel
of Your perfect plan and
Your perfect will.*

*This is love demonstrated,
love willing to stoop to do the Father's will.
For the least in the kingdom of God shall be first.*

*As I bow my knee before You,
it is Your hands that cleanse,
Your Spirit that flows through me, and
Your perfect love is shed abroad.*

> **How beautiful upon the mountain are the feet of him who brings good news.**
> **Isaiah 52:7** NKJV

Although my feet walk in this world,
my spirit soars with You,
my King.
Dancing upon the mountains of adversity,
yes, skipping upon the hills of separation
far from the valleys of strife,
uncertainty and
despair.

As my spirit dances upon the high places with You,
I am like the deer,
sure-footed upon the high places,
skipping over obstacles.

It is here that
I press my life into Yours and
look into Your eyes
that are flames of fire.
Your penetrating eyes burn from me
all that is not of You.

For You long for me to reflect Your countenance,
Your face,
Your perfect love.

I desire with all that I am to decrease
as You increase within me.

I reach out and grasp Your nail-scarred hand
        and I am reminded once again
              that You paid the price for my redemption.

Yes, You purchased me
        while I was consumed by sin and
        You breathed new life into me.

How beautiful upon the mountains are the feet of my Beloved and my Friend.

> Behold, how good and how pleasant it is
> for brethren to dwell together in unity!
> It is like the precious oil upon the head, running down.
> Psalm 133:1, 2 NKJV

My Lord, when my brother and I are not in unity
    we mar Your appearance.
        I can see that our elevated individuality
        distorts Your image, my King.

You have knitted and joined us together as one body
    with every joint supplied
      according to the effective working
        by which every part
        does its share.
And You, my Lord, You are the head
    of this many-membered body.

Yes, the oil of anointing flows from You
      to us,
      Your unified body,
  and Your life,
  Your light,
  Your love
      flows through us in full measure.

For we are a temple built by the Master's hands
in the measure of the stature of the fullness of Christ,
      and such a temple reflects Your glory.

*The whole house,
the entire temple*
        *is anointed with the same anointing oil
that flows from the head
which is Jesus.*

        *The chief spices and holy oil are compounded together
into one,
and this blessed unity flows from the unity
of the Father,
the Son
and the Spirit.*

> "He who is born in your house
> and he who is bought with your money must be circumcised,
> and My covenant shall be in your flesh for an everlasting covenant."
> **Genesis 17:13** NKJV

Look closely at your life
   and you will be able to determine
  between flesh and spirit.
Don't you know that Ishmael, the child of flesh,
became the father of twelve princes or nations?
    The counterfeit mocks the true nature or child of God,
  for Isaac also begat twelve tribes.

Twelve is the number of perfect government,
  and I desire for you first to be clothed
   in My perfection
   and My maturity.
Then, My child, you shall bring forth a great nation.

  If you eat the good of the land,
  if you eat from My table,
    you shall pay the price of total surrender.

My anointing,
 My life,
  My spirit,
   My perfection
   shall spring from you in due season.

You were a people who were not a people.
You were a foreigner.
  And you choose and you continue to choose to submit
  to the knife of circumcision.

   I continually remove your fleshly dependence
   as you submit your life unto Me.
     And My covenant shall be
     an everlasting covenant.

So rend your heart, and not your garments.
Joel 2:13 NKJV

Rend your heart and not your garment.
As you submit your will unto Me,
you can see what was so very important to you—
your proud will—
shatter and crumble before you.

Your yesterdays lie at My feet as ashes
and now you are free to pick up
and adorn yourself
with My life.
You realize that I have truly given you beauty for ashes.

It is My heart's desire that you sit with Me in heavenly places—
Yes, rule and reign with Me
for it is no longer you, My child,
that reigns upon your heart throne.

It is I who possess the gates and the very core of this city of your life.
And I reign within you.

You are a bride adorned.
Yes, you have become the new Jerusalem,
the habitation of your Lord.

You see, it was necessary
to rend your heart,
to sever the flesh from the spirit.
For no flesh shall glory in My presence in My kingdom.

As I submitted to the Father,
you also must submit and abandon all unto Me.

And My glory shall fill the temple
as your King
and Master
reigns within.

I have been crucified with Christ.
Galatians 2:20 NKJV

My beloved,
embrace the cross before you
in silence.
For as I hung upon the tree amidst cruel taunts,
I was despised
and rejected,
yet I spoke only words of love.

You, too, will face great trials and tribulation,
but it is only important how you face persecution.
I have shown you how.
Speak only words of love
and remember,
yes, cling to My promises.
For though My promises seem to tarry,
they shall be fulfilled.

I never send My word forth
or plant it into your heart
without purpose.

For in due season
My words shall blossom like the rose
and My blessings shall overtake you.
Indeed, you will not have room enough to contain Me.

May the words of your mouth
and the meditations of your heart
be always a sweet fragrance unto Me —
even in times of great distress.

Think it not strange when these fiery trials come upon you.
Embrace the cross before you
in silence
and love,
My friend.

Therefore, brethren, having boldness to enter the Holiest by the blood of Jesus, by a new and living way which He consecrated for us, through the veil, that is, His flesh, . . . let us draw near.
Hebrews 10:19, 20, 22 NKJV

May I live,
  move,
    and have my being beyond the veil,
      my Lord,
        within the most holy place.

For You have provided a way through
            the rent veil of Your flesh
            by Your precious blood.

Indeed, as I progress upon this charted path of sprinkled blood,
  I realize that You have prepared
            and made straight
                  the pathway to Your heart.
  This must be the highway of holiness
      whereupon no lion nor fierce beast may roam.
            And my pace quickens for I must
            embrace You, my King.

It is also Your blood that brings me new life.
Yes, I can even feel Your life surge through me,
for You are the Vine
and I am humbled to be a branch.

As I grow within You
and gain my sustenance from You,
the true Vine,
I realize that we are co-laborers in this peculiar garden.

You have even called me a garden enclosed
and I can see that I am covered
and clothed with
the light of Your countenance.

Now I know that I no longer need to leave Your presence
and that I may dwell forever in the house of the Lord.

> And you shall remember that the LORD your God led
> you all the way these forty years in the wilderness,
> to humble you and test you,
> to know what was in your heart,
> whether you would keep His commandments or not.
> Deuteronomy 8:2 NKJV

Lord, You have led me through the wilderness
for Your highest purpose.
>> You were progressively forming
>>> and changing me
>>>> from the image of Adam
>>>>> into the image of
>>>>>> my beloved Lord and Savior,
>>>>>>> my Jesus.

Through the testings and trials You molded within my heart humility and compassion.
>>>>> Yes, You gave me the Father's heart.

There were times You know when I could not bear the intensity of Your great love.
>> Indeed my heart would break
>>> and within that broken ground,
>>>> You would plant yet another seed of Your Spirit.

>>>> Now You have made me Your watered garden.
>>>> You dwell within this planting of the Lord.

> I have seen Your delight
> as the fruit of Your Spirit buds and springs forth.
>>>> Yes, You have made me a garden enclosed,
>>>> and the Chief Gardener,
>>>> the fairest of ten thousand,
>>>> is all glorious within.

Your Word has been my daily bread and my soul's nourishment.
> The Word of God has watered this treasure within.

Your lips drop sweetness as the honeycomb, my bride;
milk and honey are under your tongue.
The fragrance of your garments is like that of Lebanon.
Song of Solomon 4:11 NIV

*Honey and milk are under your tongue, My beloved one.
As you speak My words of life,
the Spirit flows from you
and many will receive My promises.*

*Yes, milk and honey
speak of the Promised Land
and the fullness of the Godhead dwelling within My chosen vessel.*

*For you do not draw from the ancient wells
of your tradition
and self-sufficiency,
but deep within your innermost being is a well of living water.*

*Oh, the milk and the honey of My Word,
My promises,
and all that I am through you
must flow freely from you, My child.*

*Yes, like Jonathan, even your eyes shall be enlightened and shine
with My glory.
And you shall be strengthened and reinforced
in the inner man
as you reflect your King all glorious —
yes, resident within.*

> In bringing many sons to glory,
> it was fitting that God,
> for whom and through whom everything exists,
> should make the author of their salvation perfect through suffering.
> Hebrews 2:10 NIV

I have written upon your heart, My child.
I have written with My finger,
                                      "It is finished."
Your healing and restoration have been paid for
    by the precious blood of My Son.

What was accomplished in the heavenlies shall manifest in due season.
    So look, My child, for hope in what has already been done through your Lord.

    Yes, My promises have been written
        upon your heart,
and My Word never returns empty or unfulfilled.

    I am the Word made flesh,
    and the Godhead dwells within you.

    Yes, you are My holy temple
        and I build you up brick
                    by
                brick
        with Christ Jesus as the Chief Cornerstone.

Do not look to circumstances or your own understanding —
   I only call you to trust,
         to believe,
           to have faith
   in the finished work of Jesus.

   You see, My love does not hold back.
   My love is extravagant.
                     I give you all that I am,
                     All that I have accomplished.

The plans that I have for your are for good and not for evil.
   I give you hope and a future
                     with all the promises of the Godhead.

   So rejoice, My child, for it is finished!

> But He answered and said, "It is written,
> 'Man shall not live by bread alone, but by every word
> that proceeds from the mouth of God.'"
> Matthew 4:4 NKJV

My Lord,
    You speak words of life to me
            and I gather each whisper of the Spirit
            and hold Your words to my breast.

    Indeed, I cannot live without hearing Your still, small voice.

        As I gaze into Your face,
            Your words of love rain upon my hungry and thirsty soul.
                Oh, my King, pour Your water upon
                me for I am thirsty.

                Send floods to water the dry land
                of my heart.
                Pour out Your Holy Spirit
                    fresh and anew upon me
                    this day.

Your sheep hear Your voice
and will not follow a stranger.
        I can hear You, the Chief Shepherd,
        calling me and leading me to higher ground.

Steadily You led me through the Valley of the Shadow of Death,
and I observed that it truly was but a shadow.
The things that I feared
and the enemies that surrounded me
were easily defeated by the Shepherd's
rod.

You will never,
no never
leave me or forsake me
as we continue upon this path of grace
You have chosen for me.

And because of the intimacy we share, we bring forth abundance.

> "Take my yoke upon you and learn from me,
> for I am gentle and humble in heart,
> and you will find rest for your souls.
> For my yoke is easy and my burden is light."
> Matthew 11:29,30 NIV

I do not feed you manna from yesterday.
You must eat that which has been freshly gathered.

For you are as the eagle
and you must seek with all your heart,
and you shall find your portion
for each moment.

When you began this walk with Me, My child,
you were as the ox,
forever plowing
and forever obedient,
and often faithful.

Yes, you stumbled and fell,
but I lifted you many times.

We walked together as those on the road to Emmaus
        and your eyes were opened to the yoke that we share.
In perfect symmetry we have walked, My child,
        as we plowed this field for harvest.

    I wrapped you in My love
    and fed you from My own hand.

Now, My beloved, we are not only co-laborers in the field,
        but the confines and restraints from yesterday
            have fallen as broken chains.

                And you soar as the eagle.

Now you soar with Me in higher realms
    as we turn our faces into the
            wind
          of the
        Spirit and
            rise.

> For in the day of trouble
> he will keep me safe in his dwelling;
> he will hide me in the shelter of his tabernacle
> and set me high upon a rock.
> Psalm 27:5 NIV

Put a holy watch about me, Oh Lord.
For You have made me a temple of the Holy Spirit,
and no unclean thing,
nor evil report,
nor defeated foe
may enter this habitation.

The light of Your Word
can never embrace the darkness of defeat,

for it is finished.
You have paid the
price for my victory.
The battle has
been won
and the enemy
is defeated.

Therefore, I do not possess the land,
for You, our King and Priest,
have conquered and possessed this land of
circumstances.

The prince of this world has no claim upon us,
*   as we have become the temple of habitation of the*
*   King of Kings.*
*   There is a canopy or covering about us*
*   that no evil may penetrate.*

*   Indeed, You hide us within*
*   Your heart chamber*
*   and no harm may come*
*   near us.*

Keep us in the secret place of the Most High
*   abiding in Your victorious finished work.*

> **When the enemy shall come in like a flood,
> the Spirit of the LORD shall lift up a standard against him.**
> Isaiah 59:19 KJV

I am that standard within you,
    for I am securely planted within your heart,
        and I cannot be moved.

Therefore, when the lies of the enemy would come against you
    to invade the indwelling land of promise,
        My Spirit arises within
        you to deliver you,
        to bring you from death
        to life.

    And this standard is firmly planted upon the rock.
    I shall not be moved.

For, My child, we have made a covenant
    and you are my prized possession.

My Spirit is upon you
    and I have carefully placed My words
    within your mouth
        and within the mouths of your
        descendants.

In order to do such a thing,
    I had to empty you.
        Your old selfish nature was poured out
            and with joy
                I refilled this wedding vessel
                      with new life.

And you in turn shall be poured out once again
    to offer the new wine of My Spirit.

        So, My child, as the standard or banner is a sign of danger
        or a signal for the place of assembly for Zion,
                so shall you see the enemy endangered and
                defeated
                          as we assemble or unite
                          as one.

> In the beginning was the Word, and the Word was with God,
> and the Word was God. He was in the beginning with God.
> All things were made through Him,
> and without Him nothing was made that was made.
> In Him was life, and the life was the light of men.
> John 1:1–4 NKJV

Lord, may my spirit neither slumber nor sleep
    as Your Holy Spirit consumes me.
I desire for the flame of the Spirit to continually
burn within
  as You consume all that is not of You.

As You pray within me, Holy Spirit,
    may You accomplish all for which
    You have prayed.
As You send forth Your Word,
    it always produces fruit
    and that which is the desire of
    Your heart.
      You cause my mouth to
      become a well of life.

Indeed, Your words shall return
and embrace the Godhead
  and shall not return empty.

Magnificent Lord, I once again yield my spirit and soul unto You.
  Have Your way within this temple, Oh Lord.
  May the light of the fire of Your presence never pale or diminish.

You are continually causing the Word to become flesh
  as You pour more of Yourself into me.
    And the Word becomes incarnate
    and dwells among me.

> Your servant meditates on Your statutes.
> Your testimonies also are my delight and my counselors.
> Psalm 119:23, 24 NKJV

> But we have this treasure in earthen vessels,
> that the excellence of the power may be of God and not of us.
> 2 Corinthians 4:7 NKJV

I have stored up hidden treasure in My earthen vessels.
    Yes, My hands have placed hidden manna within you
        that you may draw from the
        abundance
        within your heart.

What I give to you, My child,
    are riches the world cannot afford—
        treasures of the deep,
        words of love and life
            written upon My
            heartstrings
            that will fill the
            earth
with the knowledge and love of your Savior and King.

When you feed upon My Word,
    I store within the storehouses of your spirit more than your heart can ever contain.

*Indeed, your cup runs over
for I have filled you with living water
and fresh manna
from the chambers of My heart.*

*Spill forth the treasures of the deep within to all I put in your path.
For you can see that your steps are
ordered, guided and directed
by My own hand.*

*Sit before Me
and pour out the bounties stored
within the ocean floor of your heart.*

*For those who minister unto the King of Kings are treasures indeed.
You capture My heart
and I delight in you,
My child.*

For we who live are always delivered to death for Jesus' sake, that the life of Jesus also may be manifested in our mortal flesh.
2 Corinthians 4:11 NKJV

When you speak,
    I will be with your mouth,
        for you have believed
        and therefore you speak.
My words of life,
    healing,
    and hope
        pour from your mouth,
for I have brought forth the Spirit of My Son within you.

        Death has been working within you
        so that abundant life may now spring forth.

You have entered into the fellowship of My sufferings
    as you have died to self.

Therefore, you carry about your Savior's precious death within your body
        so that the very life of Jesus
        is manifested within you.

    Old ways are passed away.
    All things have become new.
And even though you have been crucified with Christ Jesus,
    I am faithful to raise you within Him.

You are seated in heavenly places
as My Spirit lifts you even
higher and
closer
to My heart.

Day by day you are being renewed—a new creature in Christ Jesus.

Yes, the words that I place within your mouth are Spirit and Life—
the very breath of God flows through you
to touch the nations and
to bind up the brokenhearted.

**For we are His workmanship, created in Christ Jesus for good works,
which God prepared beforehand that we should walk in them.
Ephesians 2:10 NKJV**

Yes, My child,
  you shall walk the path
  My Father has prepared for you.

  Your destiny lies before you
    as I have planned and charted your course.

There have been many times when the rocky terrain seemed too much for you to bear.
    As trials and despair came upon you,
      I was always there
        to bear your burdens
        or to lift you
      above your circumstances.

    You drank water from the rock, which is Jesus,
    and you were nurtured by My right hand.
          I was as the apple tree among the
          trees of the wild.
              You rested in My shadow
              and My fruit was your
              delight.
The desires of your heart are even now being fulfilled.

This day, My beloved, you have become a lily among thorns
    as you have become an example of My workmanship.

I have put My glory upon you
      as you climb even higher upon this holy highway to My heart.

  You see you have become a co-laborer with Christ Jesus
      since I have not only created you in Christ Jesus,
        but I also lay before you the good works
          which I have already made ready for you to accomplish.

> Drink water from your own cistern,
> and running water from your own well.
> Proverbs 5:15 NKJV

> He who believes in Me, as the Scripture has said,
> out of his heart will flow rivers of living water.
> John 7:38 NKJV

Lord, it seems as though Your holy Scriptures leap from the pages
                  to embrace my heart
                            as You open my under-
                            standing
                                to the depths of Your Spirit.

Indeed, as I feed upon Your Word,
          I can feel You write Your words of life
                    upon my heart.

As the fire of Your Spirit has burned Your promises upon my heart,
          I can now see that Your Word
          shall not return unto You empty.

I am constantly nurtured
     and fed
by this treasure within me,
               and I draw living water from the well of my spirit.

Your own hands carefully dug this well within me, my King.
        The rocks of Your Word were placed within this well of my
        spirit
                and You filled me with Your life.

Therefore, with joy I draw from the well of living water.
And I drink from that which my Master has deposited within me.

> **You are our epistle written in our hearts,
> known and read by all men.**
> **2 Corinthians 3:2** NKJV

*Unseal the book within my heart, Oh Lord,
    that Your words of life might pour forth from
        deep within.*

*I have set at Your table
    and fed from the bounty and provision
        of Your body,
            and I can feel Your Spirit
            changing me, my King.*

*For it is Your intent and heart's desire
to illuminate all that You have deposited
within this earthen vessel—
    I am progressively becoming Christ in
        and through me,
         the hope of glory.*

*My intense desire is to decrease
        so that You may increase.*

*You not only grant me the Spirit of knowledge and revelation,
    but I can feel You write Your word
    upon the tablets of my heart.*

*You are continually forming me into a living epistle
    as the fire of the Holy Spirit neither slumbers nor sleeps
    but perfects that which concerns Him.*

*You are worthy, Oh Lord, to open this book within,
    for You have redeemed me
        and made me a priest and king to my God.*

> My eyes are ever toward the LORD.
> Psalm 25:15 NKJV

As I behold Your glory, my King,
I can feel Your Holy Spirit
    adjusting,
        changing,
            cleansing,
and doing a new work within my soul.

My intellect cannot grasp this holy seed planted within
that seems to be nurtured and watered
    by Your very presence.

Beholding You,
    my countenance is changed from the image of Adam
        into Your image
    as I reflect Your face.

Indeed, the look upon my face shows or points the direction of my heart.
For my heart is ever toward You, my King.

You have not only planted Your Spirit within me;
You are also changing my very countenance
as I draw closer to You.

You are the Way or path as our faces glow with Your presence.
Therefore, let us fix our eyes upon Jesus.

Just as a runner concentrates upon the finish line,
we gaze and concentrate
upon You,
our goal and objective.

Even now we are being transformed
as we have our beginning and completion in You, my Lord.
You are the Alpha and Omega,
the beginning and the end,
and I trust You, my King,
to change me even more.

> **To everything there is a season,
> a time for every purpose under heaven.**
> **Ecclesiastes 3:1** NKJV

*Just as You placed Your hands upon Adam
                          and formed new life,
I can feel Your hands placing the seed of new life
            within me
                              to spring forth in due season.*

*You watch over Your seed of life
                as it germinates and forms within.*

*And I know that rivers of living water shall spring forth from me
                as I allow Your fruit to blossom
                as a fruit
                          out of dry ground.*

*So blow north wind of tribulation —
                        blow upon this planting of the Lord.
It shall only sink its roots deeper into
           the Word of the Lord
           and prayer without ceasing
                              will become strong and firm.*

*And the dawn of a new day shall come, my King,
                         when Your faithful little planting
                            shall spring forth
                            as the mighty
                            oak.
And this grand and glorious tree
        will bring shelter
        to the weary and heavy-laden.*

Pray without ceasing.
1 Thessalonians 5:17 NKJV

Lord, You teach my mouth to war
as Your Holy Spirit prays what is upon Your heart
through this instrument of my lips.
Often I know not what I pray
as I step into the flow of Your
Spirit
and like a mighty river,
I am swept along a course
uncharted by man.

For Your eyes sweep to and fro,
seeking for those who will enter into the Most Holy Place
and pray what is upon the heart of God.

Within me, You are ever making intercession
and I am caught up into Your manifest presence.

I know that You are gathering the prayers of the saints,
and at the appointed time
You shall pour forth this incense
upon Your people in the earth.

You have shown me that we are co-laborers as I share Your heart.
Can two walk together
unless they be as one?

Truly Your loving hands have knitted us together as one.
And as we join to present this pleasing offering and sacrifice
of intercession,
prayer,
praise
and worship unto You,
Your glory falls upon us and fills this temple.

> In the world you will have tribulation;
> but be of good cheer, I have overcome the world.
> John 16:33 NKJV

Sorrow and suffering were my companions, my Lord,
    as I walked the path prepared for
    me through this life.

Yet this cup of sorrow was not bitter, my King,
because One came alongside me to help.

    Holy Spirit, You hovered about me
        and embraced me
        with Your sweet comfort.
            I could feel You throw a blanket of
            protection and love over me.
            Your presence was a canopy about
            me
            as Your Spirit brooded and hovered
            over my weary soul.

Because You have held me in sickness and sorrow,
I can now face whatever storms tomorrow may bring.
        For I turn my face into the winds of adversity and
        cry out,
            "My God is able to do exceedingly above all that I
            ask or think."

You have conquered the enemy within and without
                and Your right hand stills the raging storm.

        You proclaim that it is finished.
        For You have paid the price of perfect peace.

Yes, my Lord, it was worth all the pain
      so that my lifetime companion,
           the Comforter,
           may embrace me.

> Every place that the sole of your foot will tread upon
> I have given you.
> Joshua 1:3 NKJV

Lord, You have brought me out
in order to bring me in.
> By the power of Your Spirit,
> I have been set free from the bondage of sin,
> > and now like a divine Joshua,
> > You lead me into a realm I have
> > not yet seen or experienced.

As You took me by the hand to lead me out,
You are now leading me by Your still small voice.
> Yes, I know You as a gentle shepherd,
> but now You stand before me as the Captain of the Host of the Lord.

In the wilderness of my past,
You provided my every need.
> Indeed, I lacked for no good thing;
> > yet within this land of
> > promise that we trod
> > there is responsibility.
> For I must appropriate the weapons of warfare that You have provided.

> Every day I do not wrestle against flesh and blood
> but against principalities and unseen powers of the dark.
> > But I am more than
> > a conqueror
> > for the Light of the
> > World
> > > rules and reigns
> > > within me.

> I can feel Your presence as we walk together as one,
> for can two walk together unless they be as one?

> Grant me fresh vision to plunge the depths of Your heart —
> > yes, keen insight into the Most Holy Place
> > as we possess the promise, my Beloved King.

> **You also, as living stones, are being built up a spiritual house, a holy priesthood, to offer up spiritual sacrifices acceptable to God through Jesus Christ.**
> **1 Peter 2:5 NKJV**

As I placed My Spirit upon the seventy elders of Moses,
he became multiplied many times.
I had created a many-membered man with one spirit
who moved in one accord.

Even so this day I look upon My many-membered body,
My end-time temple not made with hands.
For, you see, I came that you might have life
and that more abundantly.

This body of Christ is all-together lovely,
a peculiar people
and a holy nation.

For My continuous prayer is that we be one,
even as the Father and I
are one.

How beautiful upon the mountain are the feet of them who bring good news
because One came before you to bring good news.

The purpose of the anointing is to pour oil upon the head.
Yes, I am the Head,
and you are My precious body
and the oil of anointing releases My Spirit
through a chosen race,
a people who shall remove burdens and destroy yokes.

For I am the Vine
and you are the branches,
and much fruit shall abound.

**Blessed be the God and Father of our Lord Jesus Christ,
who has blessed us with every spiritual blessing
in the heavenly places in Christ.
Ephesians 1:3** NKJV

*You have walked through the wilderness
and through trials
that have put you into the fire,
and I have fortified you in the midst of tribulation.*

*But I long for you to settle within your heart
that I have enabled you to walk this path.
For I was always right there beside you.
My arms embraced you
when you were overwhelmed by
circumstances.*

*So as you set your feet into your promised inheritance which is a type of Canaan,
you notice that you are seated in heavenly places.*

*Yes, the wilderness journey has only brought about a death.
Indeed, you are dead to this world and alive in Christ Jesus—
far above any principalities,
or circumstances,
or dominion of this world
or of the enemy.*

Every place that your foot shall tread I have given unto you.
You have run and not grown weary as you sought My manifest presence,
and now we walk together as one
in newness of life in the cool of the day.

Forget those things of the wilderness,
the fires of yesterday.
Because you have been united together in the likeness of My death.
You shine forth as pure gold —
yes, as one who has been tried in the fire
and resurrected in My likeness.

The works were finished from the foundation of the world.
Hebrews 4:3 NKJV

Lord, everything You shall do,
You have already done.
You have accomplished everything before the
foundation of the world.

All of my needs have been met within Your
glorious presence.
Because I am limited by time —
and because I far too often live within this time frame —
I must lose myself within eternity,
within the realm of the eternal
for that is Your dwelling place.

You only did the works that the Father had accomplished
and in like manner we must do that which You have already
accomplished.
For we are entering a time span
where there must be no more delay between
the spoken word
and the manifested word of God.

Eternity steps into time as we acknowledge the finished work, my Lord.
The kingdom of heaven is now.
You have paid the price
and the promises have been fulfilled
before the foundation of the world.

Help me enter into Your rest;
help me believe
and have unshakable faith
within Your finished work.

For indeed, it is finished.

**It is the glory of God to conceal a matter.
Proverbs 25:2 NIV**

*Help me to search out the depths of Your Spirit, my Lord.
   Yes, may I draw from the depths of Your well
      that I might renew my mind
      and gain wisdom and understanding,
      knowledge and revelation.*

*As I draw from the living water within You, my King,
   unstop the well of my soul
      that I may freely receive Your life-giving words.*

*I choose not to deposit within my heart the
things of this world
         as I clear out
         and make straight the pathway
         to receive all You have for me this
         day.*

*As I open my heart to You,
Your eternal presence floods me and brings forth new life within.*

*Your word is pure and is a protection or shield about me both day
and night.
         Energize me once again
            as I wait before You and draw upon
            Your Spirit and Your life.*

*This is indeed my daily bread
for I can live only by every word that proceeds out of Your mouth.*

*With joy I drink Your living water and
eat the bread of life!*

> Behold, he stands behind our wall;
> He is looking through the windows, gazing through the lattice.
> Song of Solomon 2:9 NKJV

May there be no wall between us, my Lord.
As I stand face to face with You, my King,
I realize that I have constructed a middle wall or partition between us within this temple of my heart.

Only one small thread of unrepented sin,
combined with one rebellious spirit,
along with my own self-sufficiency and disobedience,
can weave this subtle veil of separation, my Beloved.

Here I stand in the holy place,
longing to remove this barrier
or whatever keeps me from entering into the fullness of my inheritance.
Through the lattice You beckon me, "Come,"
for You wait in and call me to the Most Holy Place.

You extend the scepter unto me, and my heart leaps.
Yes, You have forgiven me many times over
and You remember my sins no more.

The winter of self-condemnation is past,
and You embrace me with Your total acceptance and love.

Nothing stands between us,
as I rise up to come away with You.

> Who is this coming out of the wilderness
> like pillars of smoke,
> perfumed with myrrh and frankincense,
> with all the merchant's fragrant powders?
> Song of Solomon 3:6 NKJV

Smoke speaks of the finished work,
    for I am an all-consuming fire.

Yes, you ascend from the wilderness leaning upon Me,
    for you cannot walk without My assistance.

You see, as I did to Jacob, I have touched your strength and efforts,
    and without Me you can but limp in natural reasoning.

I have consumed you in My finished work on Calvary,
    but now My beloved, I call you
        Prince of God.

The smoke or cloud of My glory is upon you,
    for My glory shall not depart from this precious temple,
    this body consisting of many members.
        Know that this is so, for I am the
        Head of this body,
            and the oil is poured upon
            the head
            and it flows through the
            entire body —
                even unto the hem
                or finished work of the
                priest's garment.

Stand as My priest in this day —
    yes, stand in the glory,
        for I have consumed you
        and instead of ashes beauty has emerged.

**Forgetting what is behind and straining toward what is ahead,
I press on toward the goal to win the prize
for which God has called me heavenward in Christ Jesus.
Philippians 3:13b,14 NIV**

*You run and do not grow weary,
and then you walk and do not grow faint
because first you ran after Me.*

*Yes, as a deer pants for the water,
you panted after and ran towards Me.*

*And because you sought Me with all of your heart,
because you ran and did not grow weary,
you now walk with Me in the cool of the day.*

*And we share intimately the depths of our hearts
for can two walk together unless they be agreed as one?*

*You have run towards the prize of the high call in Christ Jesus,
and now, My beloved, we walk.
And every place your foot shall tread I have given unto you.*

*I surround you with favor
and I lead you beside still waters.
With each step the cares of this world fade away
and you exchange your strength for Mine.*

*Yes, My child, I look upon the heart.
Because you have longed for Me,
we walk together into eternity.*

> That I may know Him and the power of His resurrection,
> and the fellowship of His sufferings,
> being conformed to His death.
> Philippians 3:10 NKJV

I invite You to share everything with me, my Lord —
  my moments,
   my days,
   my times and
   my seasons.

May Your sweet presence integrate every hour of my life.

Because I have shared the fellowship of Your sufferings,
  You have immersed me in Your presence —
  into the intimate knowledge of You.

  A feast of love we celebrate, my Lord.
  You have spread before me a banquet table —
  yes, even a marriage supper
    as my soul and my spirit
      become one in You.

In the presence of my enemies of greed,
    self-sufficiency and
      intellect,
        You prepare this feast.

  And I find myself on the high places as I partake of You, my Beloved.

Oh, my Lord, make me ever mindful of Your holy presence
  as I lay aside the cares of this world
  and become single-visioned to look upon Your face.

For daily I am conformed to Your death,
    and together we ascend the heights of
      Your glorious resurrection.

> And the smoke of the incense, with the prayers
> of the saints, ascended before God from the angel's hand.
> Revelation 8:4 NKJV

I will take your prayers
        and commingle them with the praise and prayers of the saints,
        and this sweet incense shall ascend unto Me.

For I take great delight in the melody of your heart,
in your prayers and intercession
and in the fruit of your lips.

        As you offer unto Me the first fruits of worship,
          I gather this pleasing sacrifice unto My heart.
Can you see this holy sacrifice upon the golden altar before My throne?

      The angel takes the censer filled with this sacred fire from My altar
            and pours your prayers,
          praises
          and worship upon the earth.
                The heavens are moved
                as holiness rains upon the earth.

Light is shed abroad as you offer praise and worship,
    and I am enthroned within this pleasing offering.
            For I am the Light of the World,
            and as you are continuously filled
            with My holy fire,
                I cause you to shine —
                  to radiate My glory.

And all the earth is filled with the knowledge and the glory of the Lord.

> Lift up your heads, O you gates!
> And be lifted up, you everlasting doors!
> And the King of glory shall come in.
> Psalm 24:7 NKJV

Holy Spirit, remove my gates;
    take the barriers or gates down
        that my eyes may see You,
            the Alpha
                and the Omega.

Tear down the gate of my ears
    that I may hear Your words of spirit and life,
        as the natural world
        and the voice of the enemy dissipates
        at the sound
            of Your voice.

Oh, the words that I speak,
    let them flow like a river
        from the throne of God.

I yield the sacrifice of my lips unto You, my King;
    let Your eternal life flow through me.

Let every breath I breathe
> be the breath or wind of Your Spirit.
>> And as You tear down the gate of touch,
>> may I touch no unclean thing.

Yes, let me touch this earth and bring forth Your renewal,
> Your life,
> Your hope,
> Your strength
> and Your Spirit.

I also surrender my mind or knowledge once again, my Lord.
> I lay these dry bones of my life upon Your altar and I cry,
>> "Breathe upon me;
>> revive me once again."

> Therefore, since we are surrounded by such a great cloud of witnesses,
> let us throw off everything that hinders and the sin that so easily entangles,
> and let us run with perseverance the race marked out for us.
> Hebrews 12:1 NIV

May I outrun the chariots of the sins that so readily entangle me
with a patient endurance
and a steady persistence, my Lord.

You set before me the course or the path.
I cannot run unless You run alongside me, my Lord,
for I keep my eyes firmly fixed upon You,
the Author and Finisher of my faith!

You have brought me through much tribulation and many trials,
but in this race You have clothed me with the garment of praise
as I surrender the spirit of heaviness.

For the joy set before You,
You paid the price that I might be clothed in You.
Yes, I've exchanged the old man
for this spotless garment of righteousness.

The mystery truly is Christ in and through me,
the hope of glory.

And as we run, my King,
>*I can see that we are seated in heavenly places.*
>>*The eyes of my understanding are enlightened*
>>*and I comprehend the hope of that You have called me to.*

Somewhere in the running of this race set before me,
>*I died*
>>*and my life is hidden with You, my King.*
>>*You have made me a co-heir*
>>*to rule and reign with You.*

Without You,
>*I can do nothing*

but with You,
>*I can do all things through Christ Jesus.*

> Our fathers disciplined us for a little while as they saw best;
> but God disciplines us for our good,
> that we may share in his holiness.
> Hebrews 12:10 NIV

I have written upon your heart, My child,
I have written with My fingers:
"It is finished."

Your healing and restoration has been paid for by the precious blood of My Son.

What was accomplished in the heavenlies
shall manifest in due season.
So, My child, look for
hope in what has already been done
through your Lord.

Yes, My promises have been written upon your heart,
and My Word never returns empty or unfilled.
I am the Word made flesh,
and the Godhead dwells within you.

Yes you are My holy temple
and I build you up brick by brick
with Christ Jesus as the Chief Cornerstone.

Do not look to circumstances or your own understanding.
I call you only to trust and believe,
*   to have faith in the finished work of Jesus.*

You see, My love does not hold back.
*   My love is extravagant.*
*   I give you all that I am —*
*   all that I have accomplished.*

The plans that I have for you are for good and not for evil.
*   I give hope and a future*
*   with all the promises of the Godhead.*

*   So rejoice, My child, for it is finished!*

> [The Father] has delivered and drawn us to Himself
> out of the control and the dominion of darkness
> and has transferred us into the kingdom of the Son of His love.
> Colossians 1:13 AMP

Father,

    I rest in Your perfect love.
    For You have drawn me into the kingdom of the Son of Your love.

    As I am securely nestled within Jesus,
        I can see that all of my needs and concerns are met.
        Indeed, Jesus has already paid the price
            and His blood cries out from the finished
            work of the cross.

    I have entered Your perfect rest through the freshly slain Lamb of God,
        for the blood of Jesus is just as fresh and powerful
            as it was two thousand years ago.

It is Your earnest desire that I share in the inheritance of the saints,
    for You have drawn me to Your side
        out of the control and dominion of darkness
            into my beloved Jesus.

Therefore,
    within my heart I have built an altar to You, my Lord,
    and each day I sacrifice my own will,
        my own mind and
        my own walk
            unto the One True God.
    This joyful surrender frees my spirit to soar in the heavenly places,
        for he that is joined to the Lord is one.

    This corruptible shall put on incorruptible
        and this mortal shall put on immortality.

    The two of us become one within Your perfect love.

> **You shall be like a watered garden.**
> **Isaiah 58:11** NKJV

Plow up my heart, Oh Lord,
                                to receive the seed of Your Word.
                                I ask You to watch over and protect
                                that which You have planted.

                                May the little foxes of this earthly life not
                                spoil the vine,
                                for You are the True Vine.

Give me understanding
        so that the enemy will not snatch away
        what You have so carefully placed within my heart.

Let me not become as the stony ground,
        joyfully receiving Your Word without the deep roots
        penetrating through tribulation
                and that which would destroy this most holy seed.

You have made me to be a lily among thorns;
        therefore, I protect and nourish Your Word
                as the cares of this world would choke the Word.
                May the thorns of this life never destroy the seed
                                within my heart.

For You,
>	and You alone,
>>	carefully placed Your words of life within my spirit.
>	By Your own hand
>>	You shelter me
>>	that in due season I may bring forth thirty,
>>>	sixty,
>>>	and a hundred fold,
>>>>	precious fruit to delight
>>>>	Your heart —
>>>>	fruit in abundance
>>>>	to make Your heart glad.

And as You partake of that which is within me,
>	may I rise into You once more,
>>	that You may put Your hand to the plow
>>	only to plant again.

And our hope for you is firm,
because we know that just as you share in our sufferings,
so also you share in our comfort.
2 Corinthians 1:7 NIV

I am this day uncapping our well of living water.
No longer shall you be a spring shut up
or a fountain sealed.

For I am the living water that must nourish and strengthen all flesh.
And when you partake of Me,
you are filled with all the fullness of the Godhead.

Even now you are emerging from the dry wilderness
of trials and testing.

Your garments never wore out,
for you are adorned with my
righteousness.

For by gazing into the mirror of My Word,
you see with the eyes of your spirit,
and you have been changed
into My image.

Yes, it is I who bring you from
glory to glory.

Finally, my love, you rested upon the palanquin
    of My protection and love.
        You can never walk with your own purpose
        or your own will, My beloved,
            for you would stumble
            and fall.

It's only when you allow Me to carry you
    that you overcome.
    I am the Great High Priest that carries
    you upon My shoulders.

So spring up, oh well of living water;
    for the winter is past.
    The time for rejoicing has come.

As you have partaken of sufferings,
    so also do you now partake of the consolation.

> A garden enclosed is my sister, my spouse,
> a spring shut up, a fountain sealed.
> Song of Solomon 4:12 NKJV

As Jacob rolled the stone away from the well to water the sheep of Rachael,
    so, my Lord, do You roll the barrier or stone from my heart
        that Your living water may flow forth.

Rend the veil within my soul,
    and let Your Holy Spirit flow where You please.
    For it is You, and You alone,
        who guards my heart.
        I am a spring shut up
        and a fountain sealed
            until You release Your
            life within me.

Come to Your well of living water, my King.
Come and partake of the Christ nature within,
    for I am nothing of myself.
        But I am a tabernacle;
        I contain the well of life.

Drink freely of my worship,
    my adoration,
    my love for You,
        my Beloved.

Roll away any stones of hesitation or self,
    and may Your life-giving water flow from the depths of my being.

> Come, and let us return to the LORD;
> for He has torn, but He will heal us.
> Hosea 6:1 NKJV

Rend your heart,
        and not your garment,

        as you submit your will unto Me.
        You can see what was so very important to you—
            your proud will—
        shatters and crumbles before you.

    Your yesterdays lie at My feet as ashes,
        and now you are free to pick up and adorn yourself
            with My life.
            You realize that I have
            truly given you
                beauty
              for
            ashes.

    It is My heart's desire that you sit with Me
        in heavenly places,
            yes, rule and reign with Me
            for it is no longer you, My
            child,
                that reigns upon your
                heart throne.
                It is I who possess the gates
                and the very core of
                this city of your life.
                And I reign within
                you.

You are as a bride adorned.
Yes, you have become the new Jerusalem,
        the habitation of your Lord.

You see, it was necessary to rend your heart,
        to sever the flesh from the spirit.
              For no flesh shall glory in My presence in My kingdom.

        As I submitted to the Father,
        you also must submit
               and abandon all to Me.

And My glory shall fill the temple
              as your King and Master reigns
              within.

> O Lord, open my lips,
> And my mouth shall show forth Your praise.
> Psalm 51:15 NKJV

In all your ways acknowledge Me as I direct your paths —
yes, even in the difficult and impossible circumstances.

Raise your voice in praise and watch as I inhabit your praises.
I am enthroned within the situation
for you are My precious temple,
and flesh cannot stand in My presence.

As we continue in one accord,
the enemy is totally defeated.
As you lean not to your own understanding,
we are not moved by what we see, My love.

As you become immersed in worship,
you notice that, having left the outer court of the natural
and the inner court of praise or thanksgiving,
you find yourself in the Most Holy Place of
worship and abandonment.

You stand face to face with Me.
Oh, My child, remove the shoes of your manmade efforts
for the ground whereon you stand is holy ground.

**Trust in the LORD with all your heart,
And lean not on your own understanding.
Proverbs 3:5 NKJV**

*In the valley of affliction
You have kept me, my Lord.
   I can feel Your healing hands hold my head
   as You take away the pain.
     You whisper words of love to soothe me,
     and I slowly surrender my pain
       as I exchange my weakness
       for Your strength.*

*Yes, You have sustained me in my darkest hour.
   It's not important that I go through the storms and
   tempests of life.
   It's only important that You are faithful,
     that You will sustain me,
     that Your grace is
     sufficient.*

*   Therefore, I shall not fear
     for You have brought me far
     above my afflictions, far
     above the cares of this life,
     and I know that You hold the
     universe
       in Your hands.*

*You are the God of all flesh
   and nothing — no, nothing —
     is too difficult for You.*

> **Those who trust in the Lord are like Mount Zion,
> which cannot be moved,
> but abides forever.**
> **Psalm 125:1 NKJV**

I have made you to be as Mt. Zion
  as you trust in Me.
And as the mountains are around Jerusalem,
  so am I around you,
  shielding and protecting you
  from all harm.

You, like Mt. Zion, cannot be moved
  for your heart is fixed trusting in Me.

In the midst of circumstances,
  lift up your eyes and behold your King.
    I am the very breath that you breathe.
    I give perfect peace all the days of your life
    as you keep your eyes firmly fixed on Me.
    The waters of the cares of this life shall not
    overwhelm you.

As you put your trust in Me,
  your soul has been liberated
  as a bird set free from the snare of the fowler.
  I have broken the snare of sin,
    sickness
    and death.

Mt. Zion cannot be moved.
  I surround you with protection,
    favor,
    and perfect love.

**And the Lord God formed man of the dust of the ground,
and breathed into his nostrils the breath of life;
and man became a living being.
Genesis 2:7 NKJV**

May I praise and worship You
        with the very breath You breathed into me,
            my Lord.

You gave of your own breath that man became a living being,
    and now I can feel the wind of Your Spirit
        bring forth new and fresh life within.

The disappointments of life pale in comparison to You, my Lord.
    For when I am weary and heavy-laden,
        I come into the Most Holy Place;
        I run to You,
        and Your presence,
        Your great love embraces
        me.

        I cast my cares upon You,
            for You are able to lift me
            far above the circum-
            stances.
            And I emerge from the
            wilderness of the soulish
            realm to soar in heav-
            enly places.

You have changed my name to "prince of God,"
   and I limp as one who has truly
   been touched
      by the living God.

   For I depend on You.
   There is nothing I can accomplish
   or achieve
      unless You flow through
   me.

You are the Vine,
I am the branch,
   and You came for the poor in spirit,
      the lame
      and the halt.

Other books written by Anne Wampler:

Look Only to Me

The Father's Heart

Living Water or
Agua Viva (Spanish Version)

The Voice of My Beloved

**To order, please send $9.00 per book or $30.00
for all four books
(Indicate Spanish or English version of** *Living Water*)
plus $3.00 S & H for one book, add another $1.00 for each additional book
to:

Anne Wampler
5261 South Stonehaven Drive
Springfield, MO 65809

Email the author at annewampler@mchsi.com

To order additional copies of

GOLD
FROM THE

Have your credit card ready and call

Toll free: (877) 421-READ (7323)

or send $10.00** each plus $4.95 S&H* to

WinePress Publishing
PO Box 428
Enumclaw, WA 98022

or order online: www.winepresspub.com

**WA residents, add 8.4% sales tax

*add $1.00 S&H for each additional book ordered